GRAPHIC HISTORY

LORDS OF THE SEA

THE VIKINGS EXPLORE THE NORTH ATLANTIC

by Allison Lassieur
illustrated by Ron Frenz
and Charles Barnett III

Consultant:
Roland Thorstensson, PhD
Professor of Scandinavian Studies and Swedish
Gustavus Adolphus College
St. Peter, Minnesota

Capstone press

Mankato, Minnesota

Graphic Library is published by Capstone Press,
151 Good Counsel Drive, P.O. Box 669, Mankato, Minnesota 56002.
www.capstonepress.com

Printed in the United States of America

1 2 3 4 5 6 10 09 08 07 06 05

Library of Congress Cataloging-in-Publication Data
Lassieur, Allison.
Lords of the sea: the Vikings explore the North Atlantic / by Allison Lassieur; illustrated by Ron Frenz and Charles Barnett III.
p. cm.—(Graphic library. Graphic history)
Summary: "In graphic novel format, tells the story of the Vikings' exploration of the North Atlantic Ocean"—Provided by publisher.
Includes bibliographical references and index.
ISBN 0-7368-4974-2 (hardcover)
1. Vikings—Juvenile literature. 2. Vikings—Comic books, strips, etc.—Juvenile literature. 3. North America—Discovery and exploration—Norse—Juvenile literature. 4. North America—Discovery and exploration—Norse—Comic books, strips, etc.—Juvenile literature. I. Barnett, Charles, III ill. II. Frenz, Ron ill. III. Title. IV. Series.
DL65.L374 2006
948'.022—dc22 2005007891

Art and Editorial Direction
Jason Knudson and Blake A. Hoena

Designer
Jason Knudson

Colorist
Benjamin Hunzeker

Editor
Christopher Harbo

TABLE OF CONTENTS

CHAPTER 1

THE VIKING SPIRIT OF ADVENTURE

In the AD 700s, the Vikings lived in Scandinavia. This area included the present-day countries of Norway, Sweden, and Denmark. Most Vikings lived in small villages along the coast and made their livings as farmers.

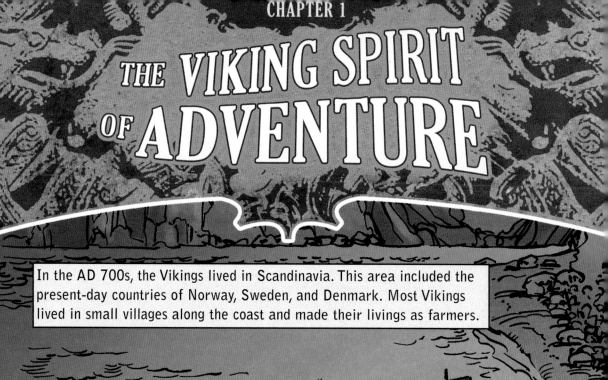

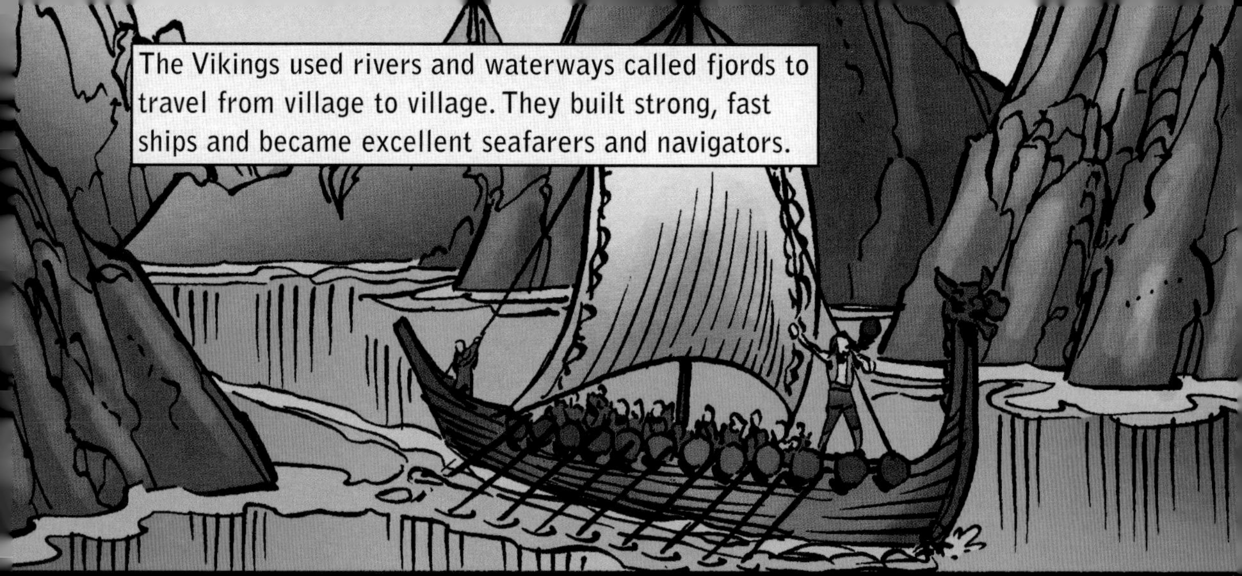
The Vikings used rivers and waterways called fjords to travel from village to village. They built strong, fast ships and became excellent seafarers and navigators.

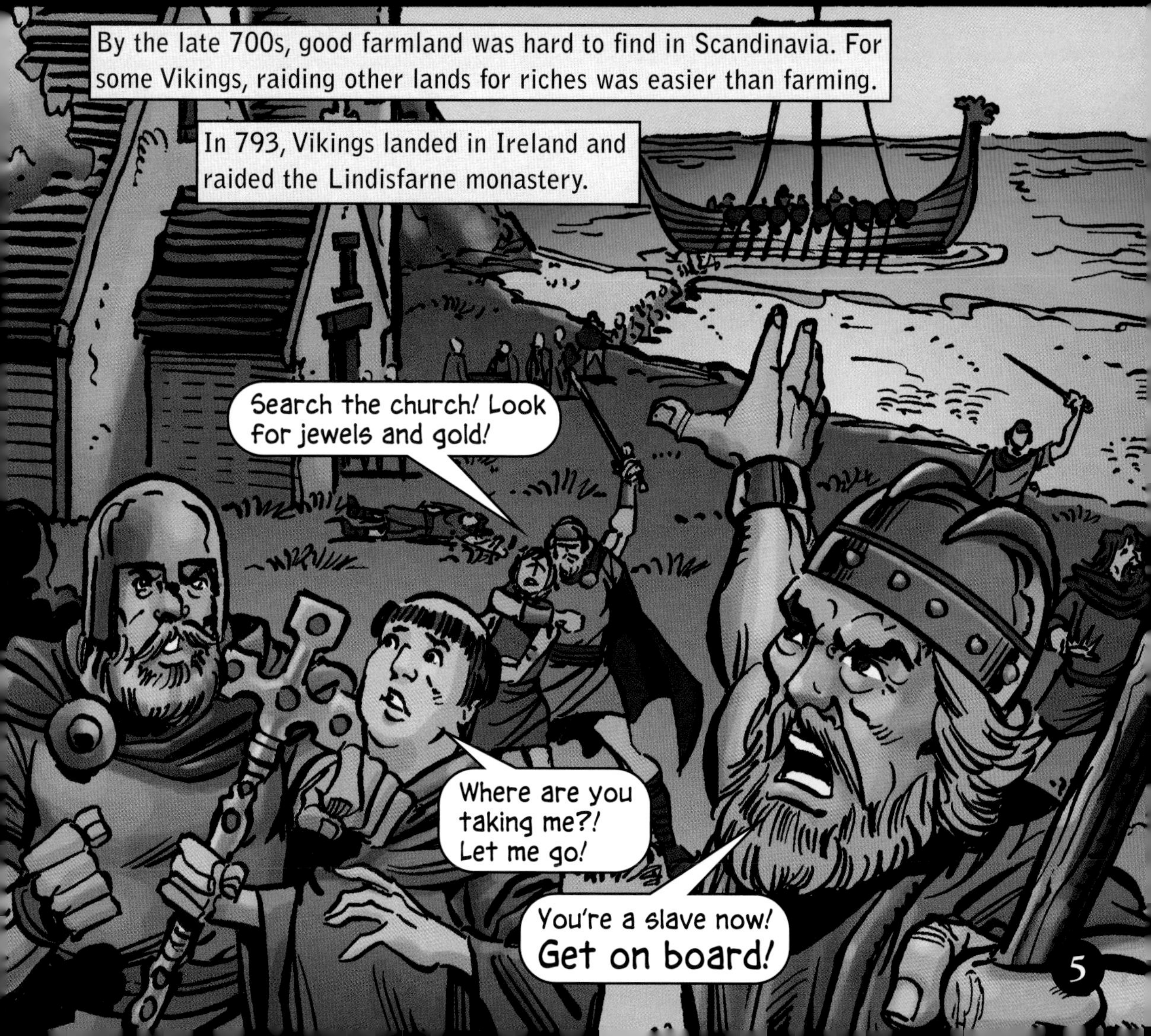
By the late 700s, good farmland was hard to find in Scandinavia. For some Vikings, raiding other lands for riches was easier than farming.
In 793, Vikings landed in Ireland and raided the Lindisfarne monastery.
Search the church! Look for jewels and gold!
Where are you taking me?! Let me go!
You're a slave now! Get on board!

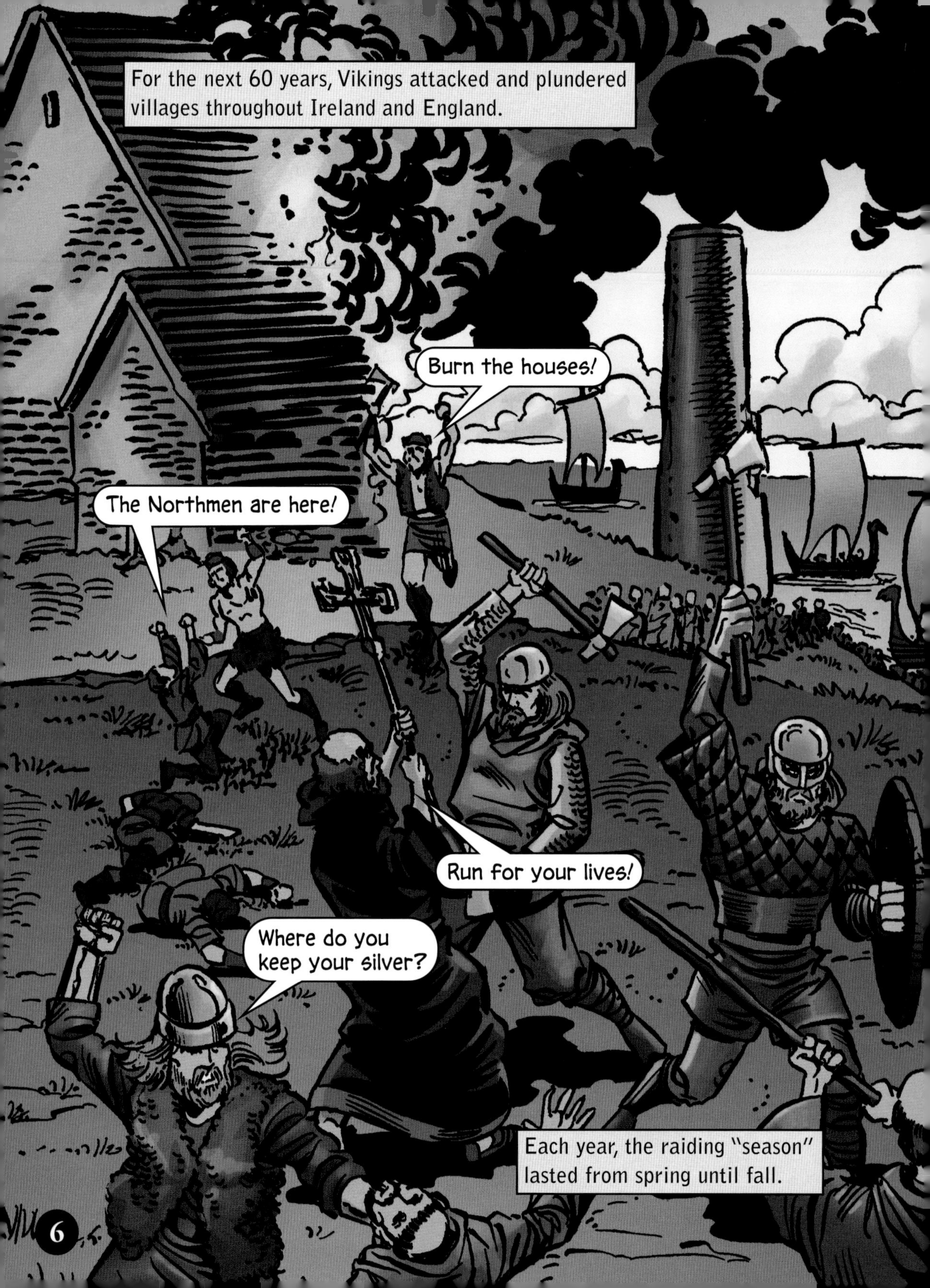
For the next 60 years, Vikings attacked and plundered villages throughout Ireland and England.
Burn the houses!
The Northmen are here!
Run for your lives!
Where do you keep your silver?
Each year, the raiding "season" lasted from spring until fall.

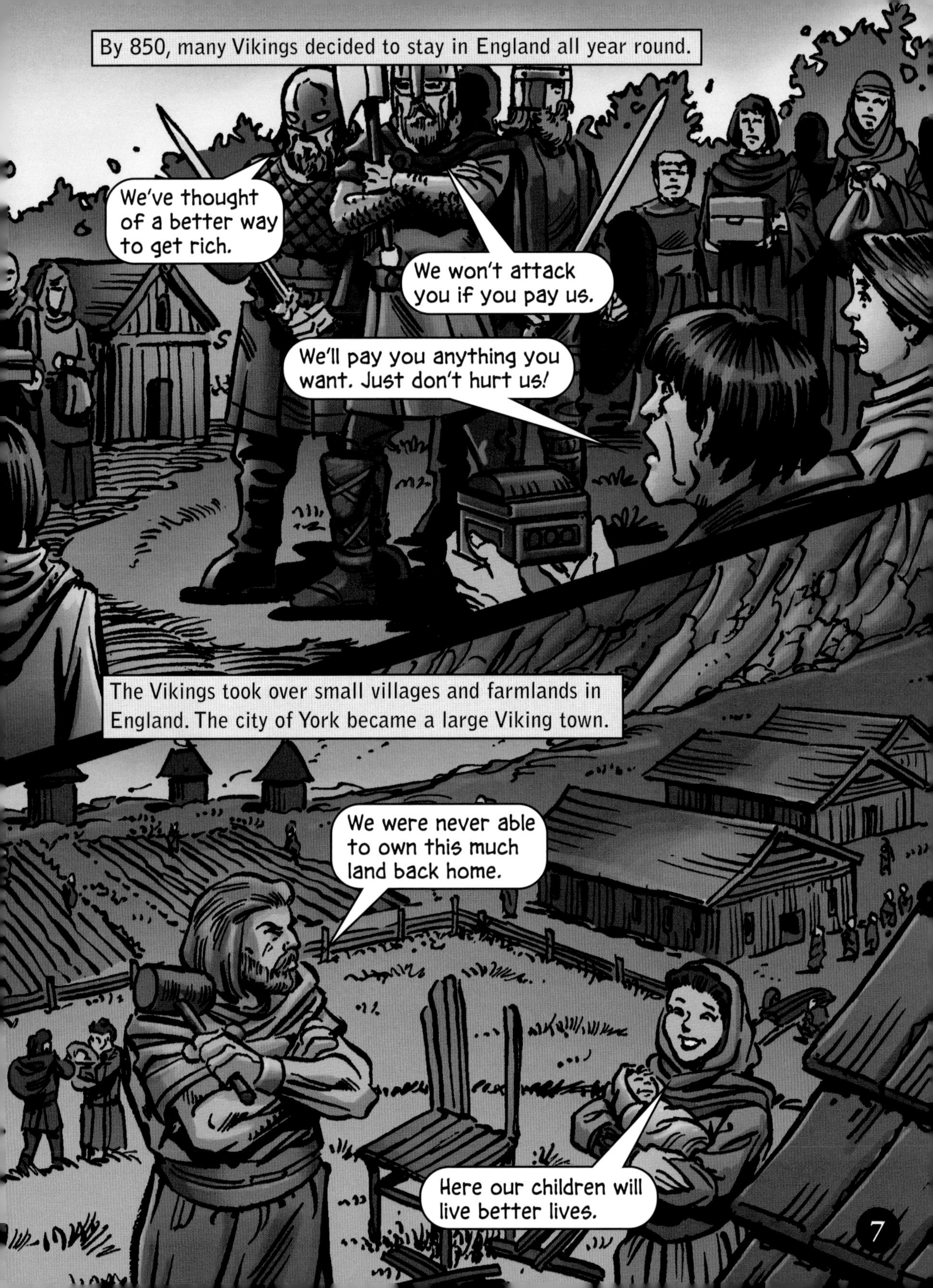
By 850, many Vikings decided to stay in England all year round.
We've thought of a better way to get rich.
We won't attack you if you pay us.
We'll pay you anything you want. Just don't hurt us!
The Vikings took over small villages and farmlands in England. The city of York became a large Viking town.
We were never able to own this much land back home.
Here our children will live better lives.

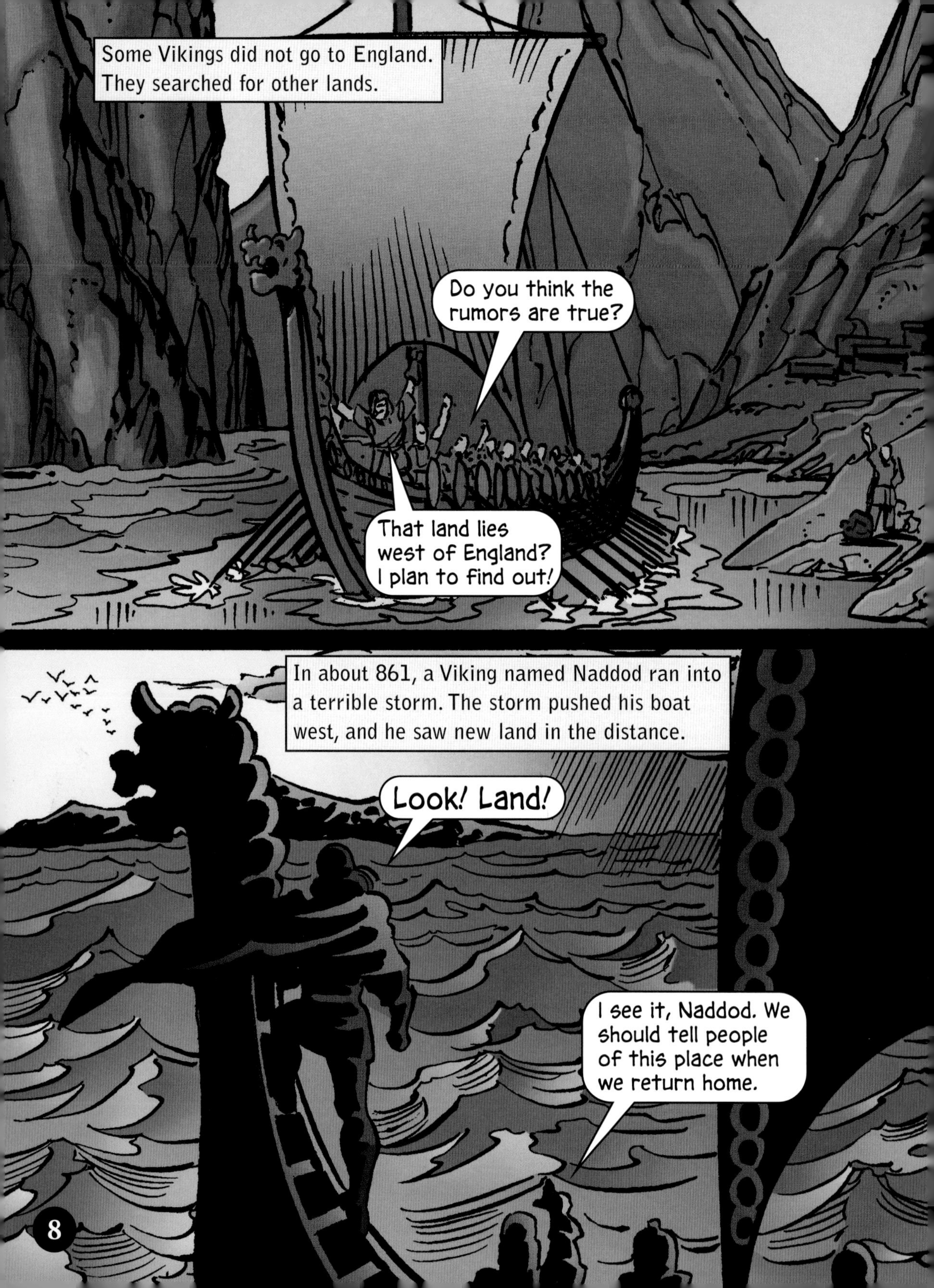
Some Vikings did not go to England. They searched for other lands.
Do you think the rumors are true?
That land lies west of England? I plan to find out!
In about 861, a Viking named Naddod ran into a terrible storm. The storm pushed his boat west, and he saw new land in the distance.
Look! Land!
I see it, Naddod. We should tell people of this place when we return home.

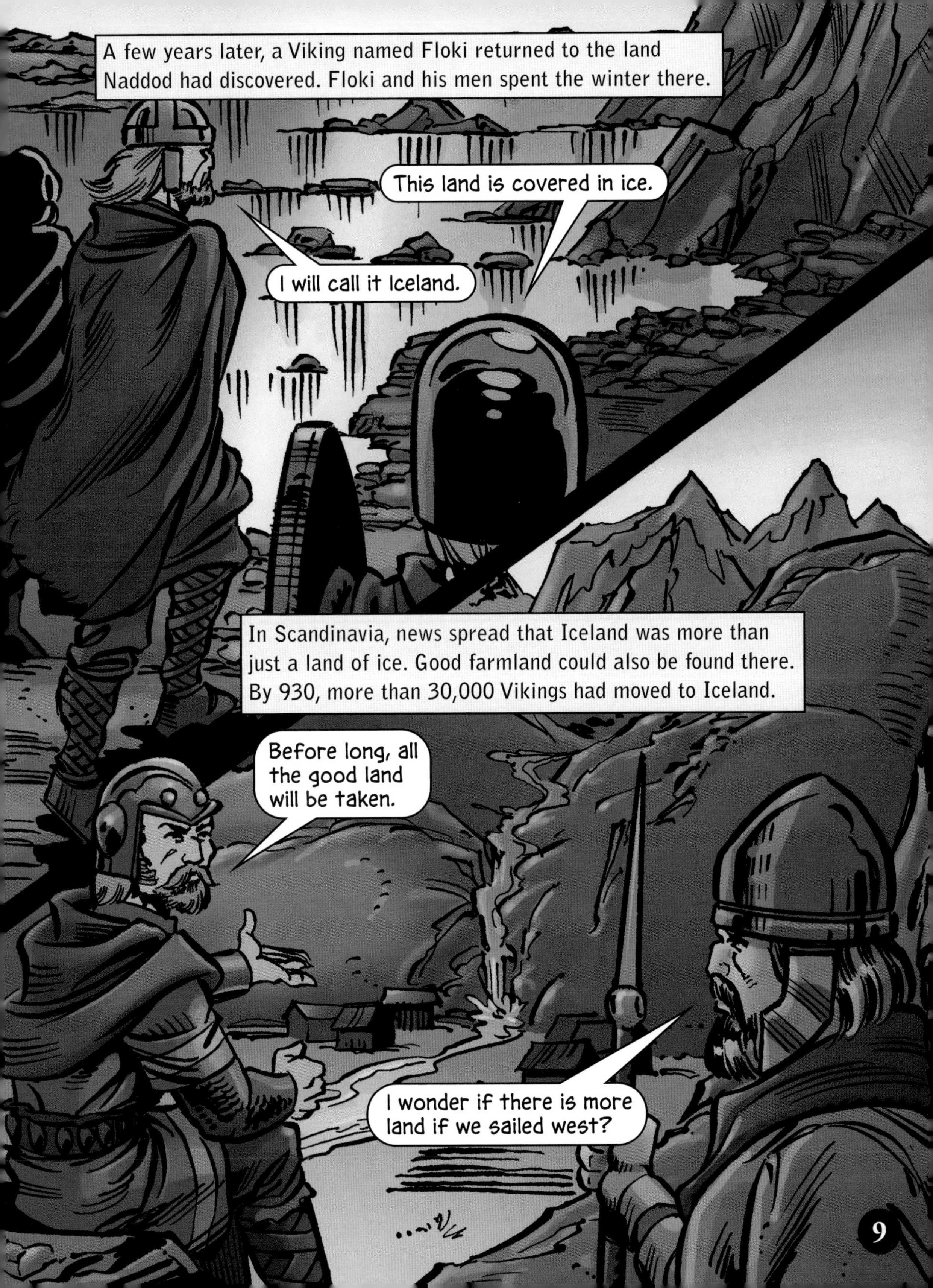
A few years later, a Viking named Floki returned to the land Naddod had discovered. Floki and his men spent the winter there.
This land is covered in ice.
I will call it Iceland.
In Scandinavia, news spread that Iceland was more than just a land of ice. Good farmland could also be found there. By 930, more than 30,000 Vikings had moved to Iceland.
Before long, all the good land will be taken.
I wonder if there is more land if we sailed west?

CHAPTER 2

EXPLORING THE NORTH ATLANTIC

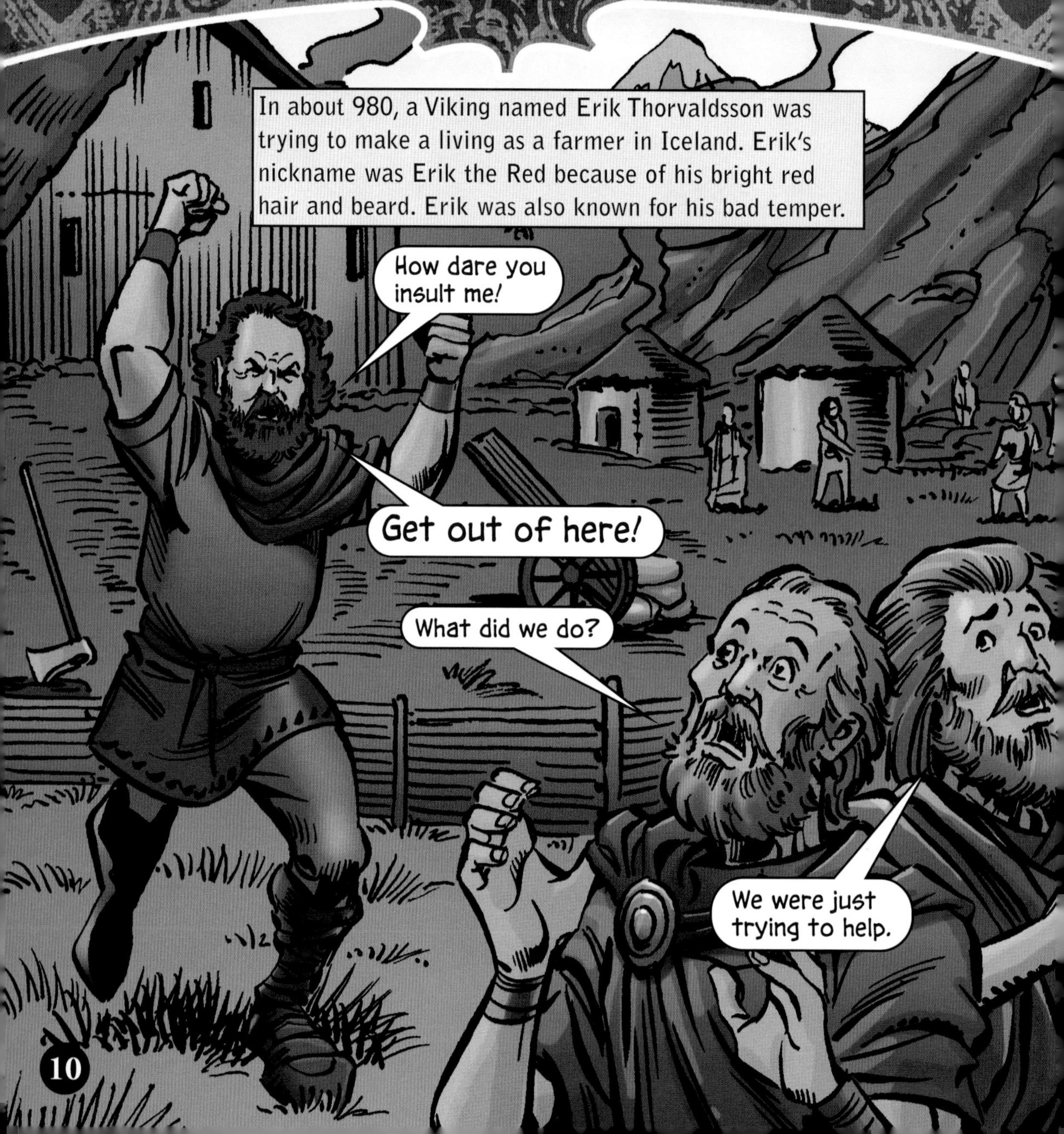
In about 980, a Viking named Erik Thorvaldsson was trying to make a living as a farmer in Iceland. Erik's nickname was Erik the Red because of his bright red hair and beard. Erik was also known for his bad temper.
How dare you insult me!
Get out of here!
What did we do?
We were just trying to help.

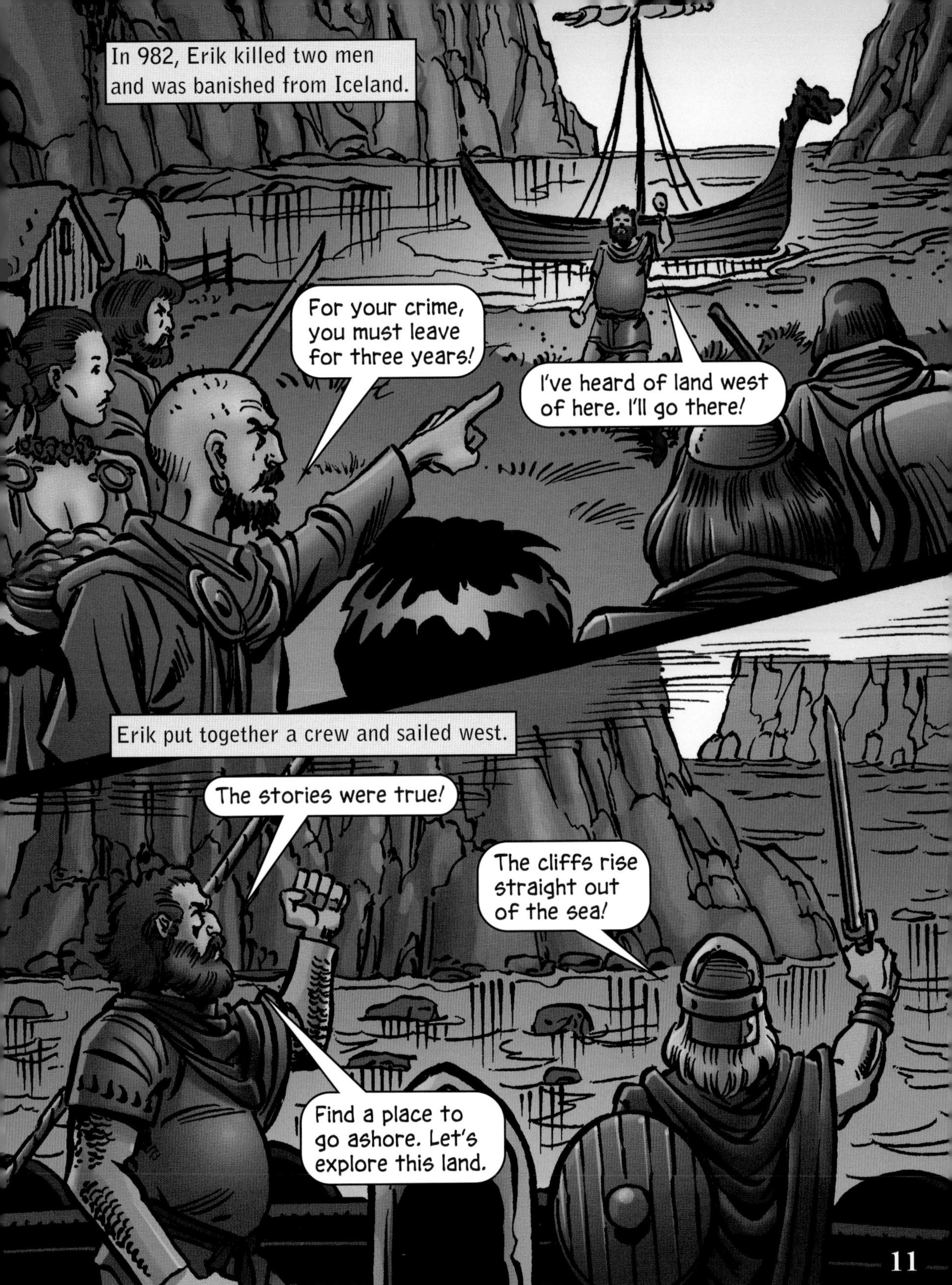
In 982, Erik killed two men and was banished from Iceland.
For your crime, you must leave for three years!
I've heard of land west of here. I'll go there!
Erik put together a crew and sailed west.
The stories were true!
The cliffs rise straight out of the sea!
Find a place to go ashore. Let's explore this land.

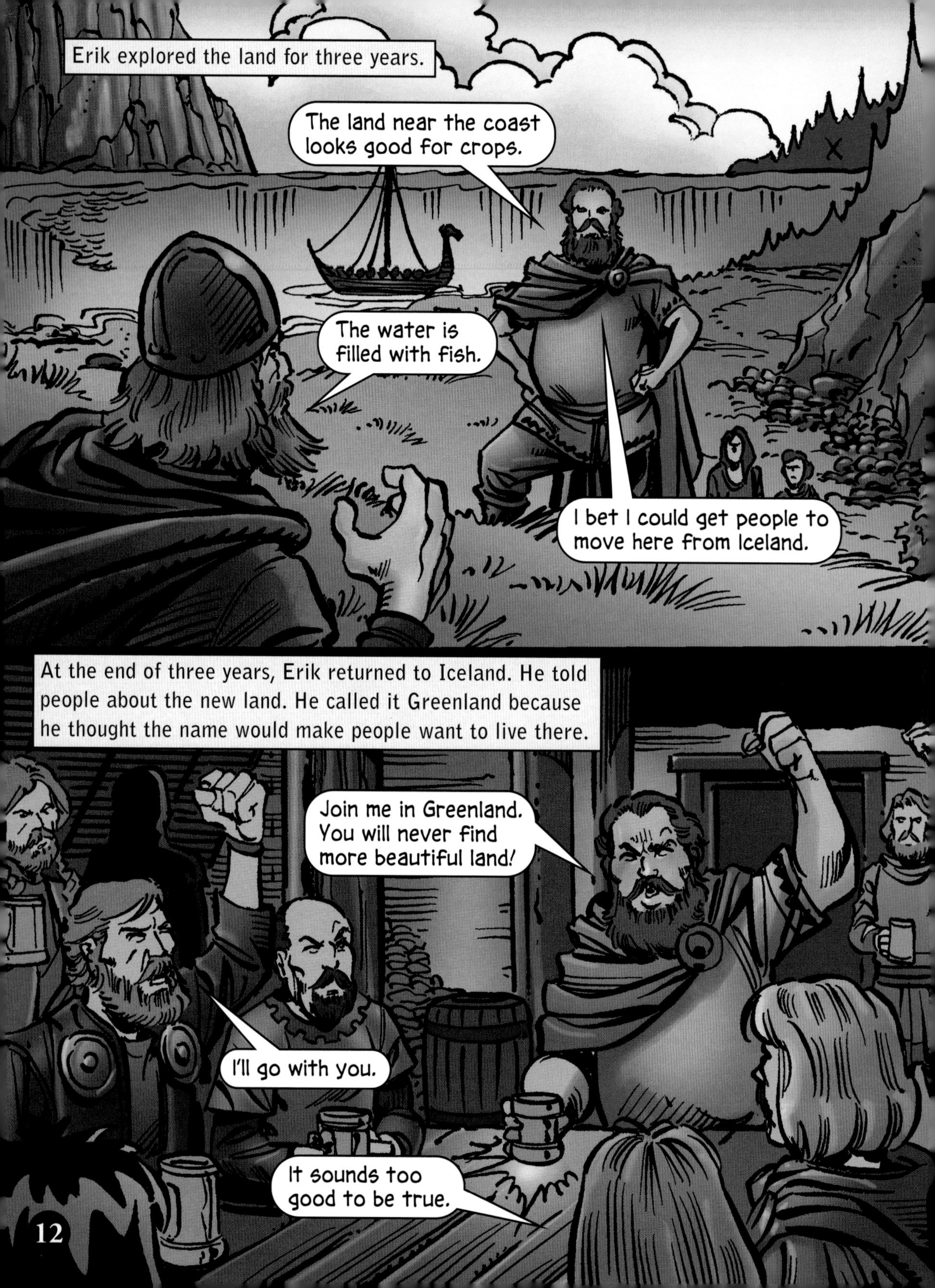
Erik explored the land for three years.
The land near the coast looks good for crops.
The water is filled with fish.
I bet I could get people to move here from Iceland.
At the end of three years, Erik returned to Iceland. He told people about the new land. He called it Greenland because he thought the name would make people want to live there.
Join me in Greenland. You will never find more beautiful land!
I'll go with you.
It sounds too good to be true.

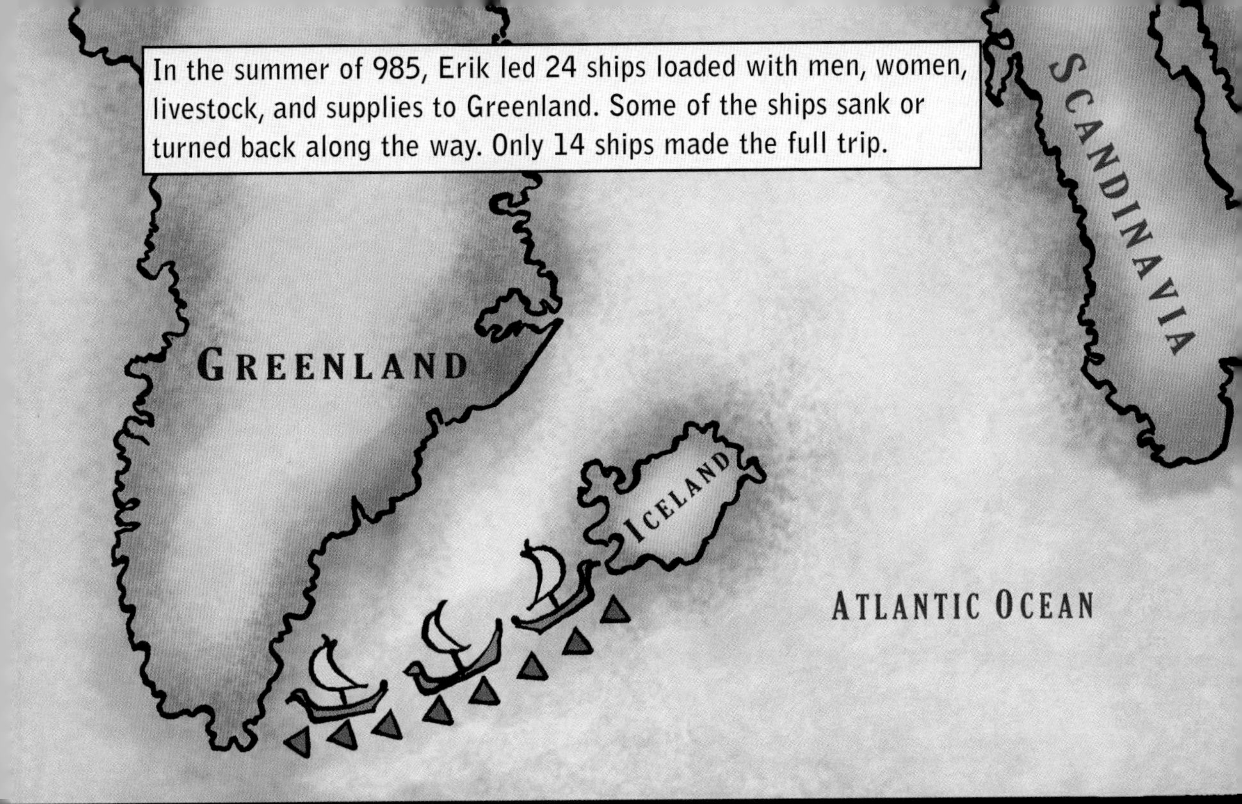
In the summer of 985, Erik led 24 ships loaded with men, women, livestock, and supplies to Greenland. Some of the ships sank or turned back along the way. Only 14 ships made the full trip.
GREENLAND
SCANDINAVIA
ICELAND
ATLANTIC OCEAN

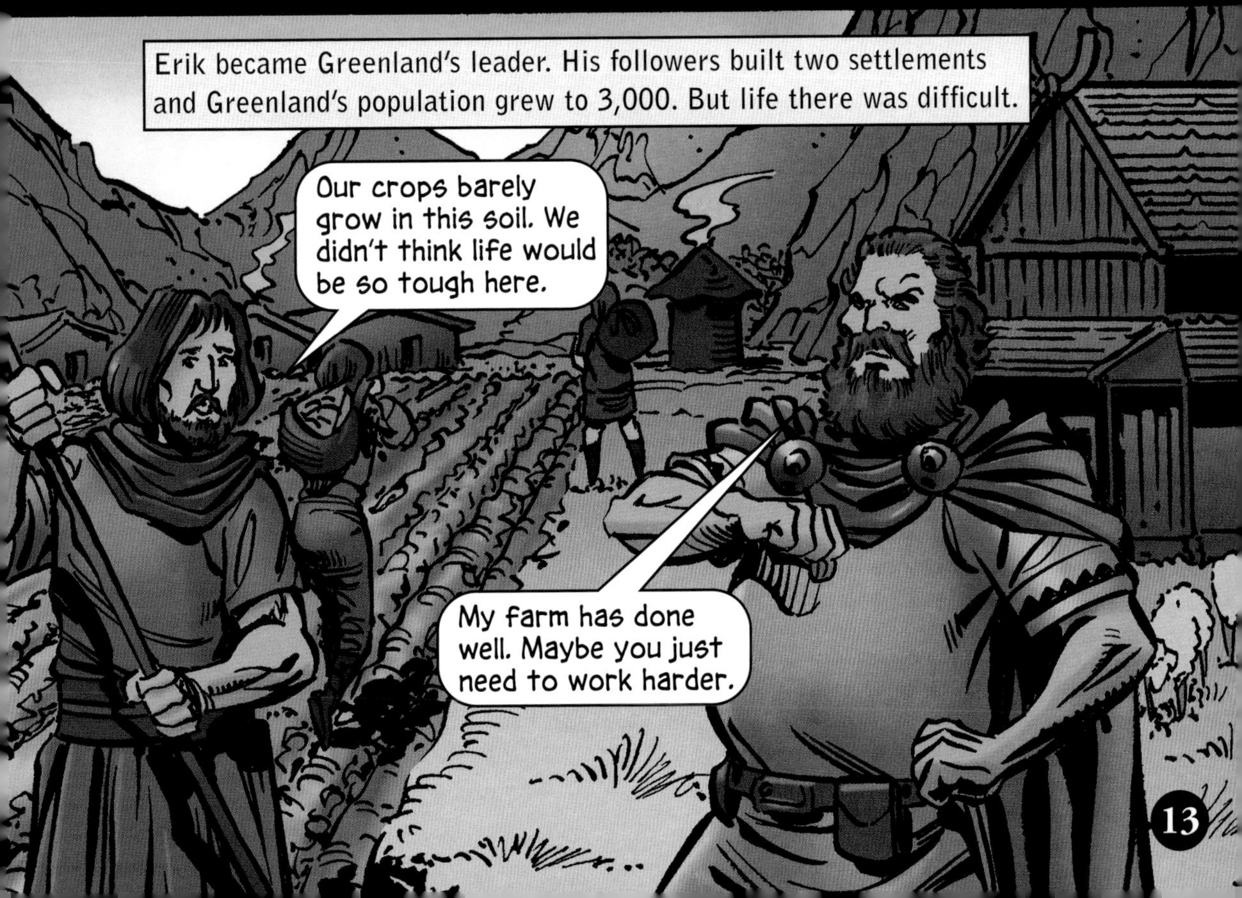
Erik became Greenland's leader. His followers built two settlements and Greenland's population grew to 3,000. But life there was difficult.
Our crops barely grow in this soil. We didn't think life would be so tough here.
My farm has done well. Maybe you just need to work harder.

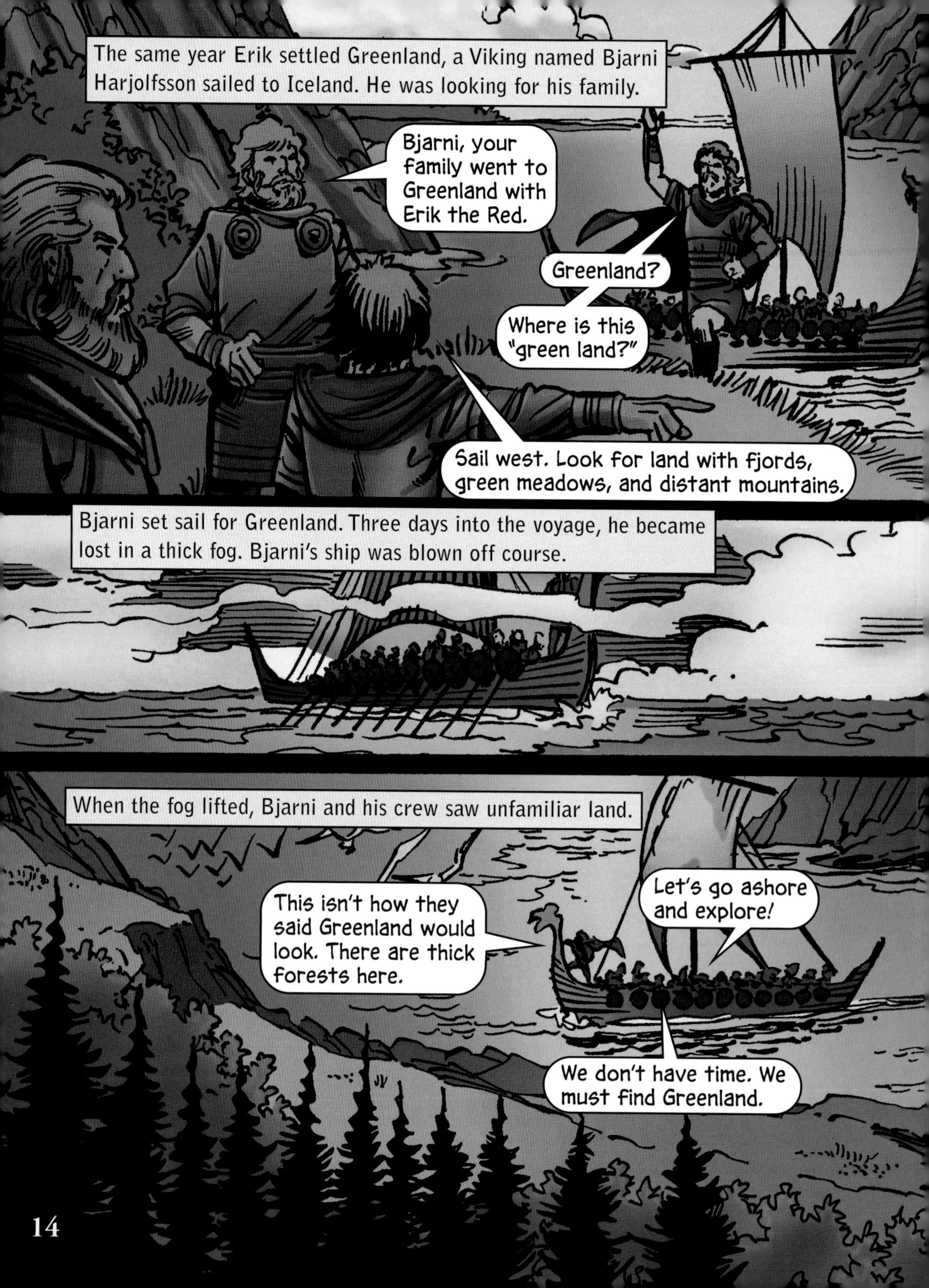
The same year Erik settled Greenland, a Viking named Bjarni Harjolfsson sailed to Iceland. He was looking for his family.
Bjarni, your family went to Greenland with Erik the Red.
Greenland?
Where is this "green land?"
Sail west. Look for land with fjords, green meadows, and distant mountains.
Bjarni set sail for Greenland. Three days into the voyage, he became lost in a thick fog. Bjarni's ship was blown off course.
When the fog lifted, Bjarni and his crew saw unfamiliar land.
This isn't how they said Greenland would look. There are thick forests here.
Let's go ashore and explore!
We don't have time. We must find Greenland.

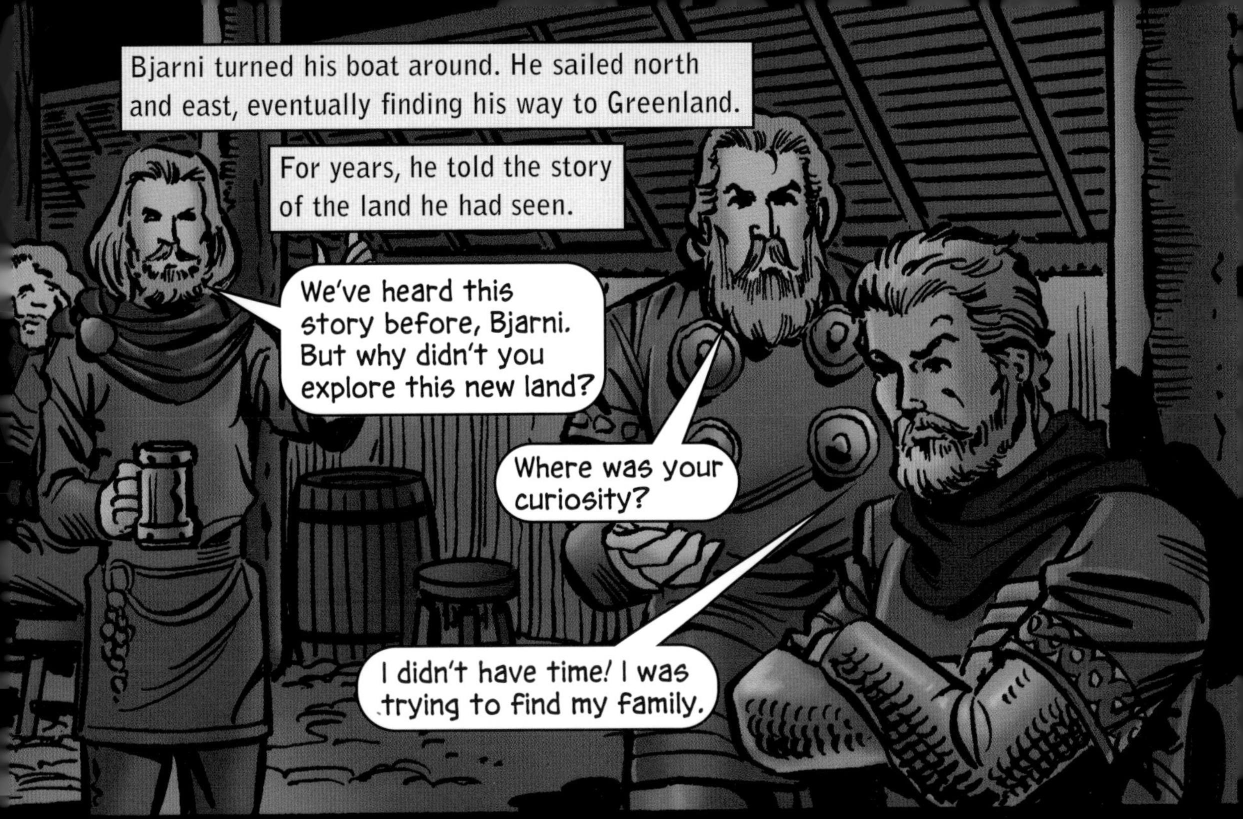
Bjarni turned his boat around. He sailed north and east, eventually finding his way to Greenland.
For years, he told the story of the land he had seen.
We've heard this story before, Bjarni. But why didn't you explore this new land?
Where was your curiosity?
I didn't have time! I was trying to find my family.

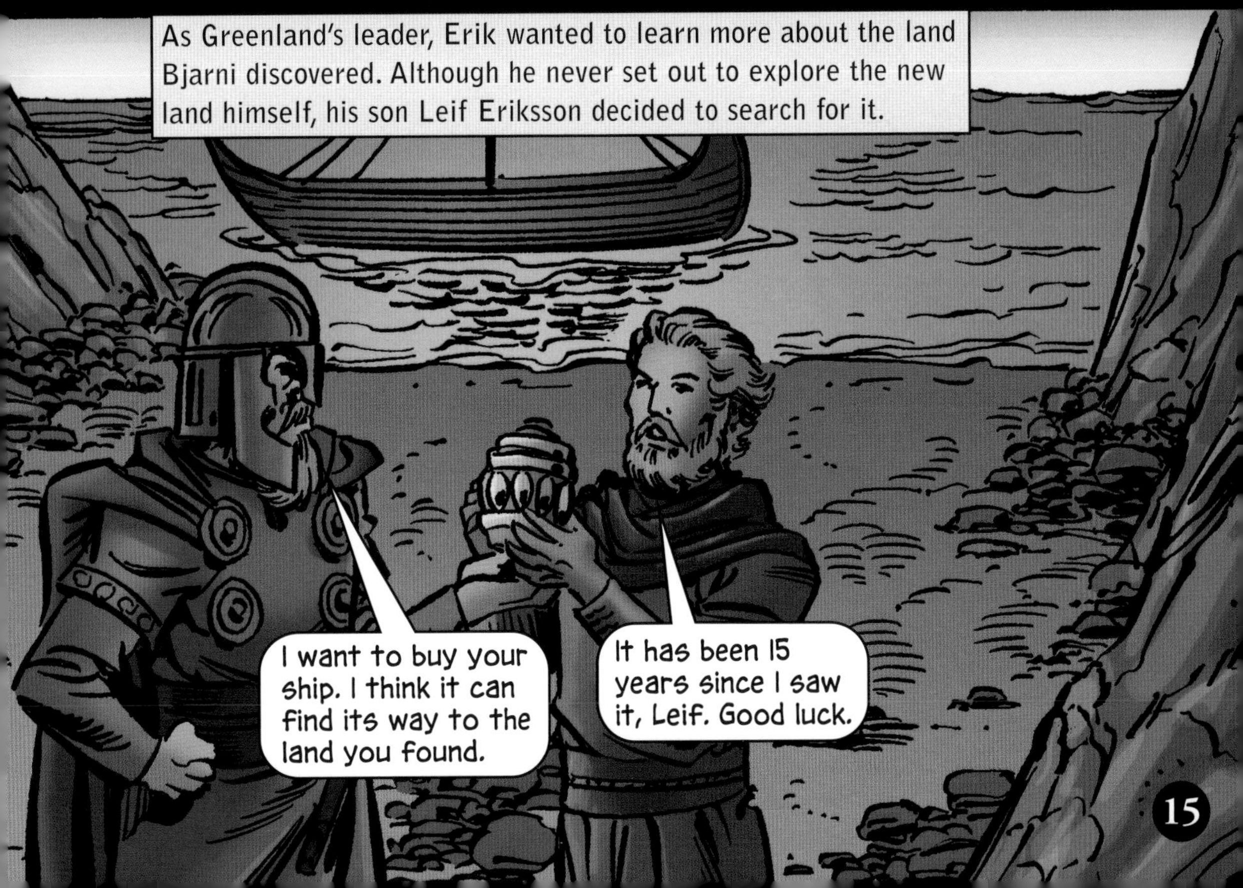
As Greenland's leader, Erik wanted to learn more about the land Bjarni discovered. Although he never set out to explore the new land himself, his son Leif Eriksson decided to search for it.
I want to buy your ship. I think it can find its way to the land you found.
It has been 15 years since I saw it, Leif. Good luck.

CHAPTER 3

VIKINGS DISCOVER NORTH AMERICA

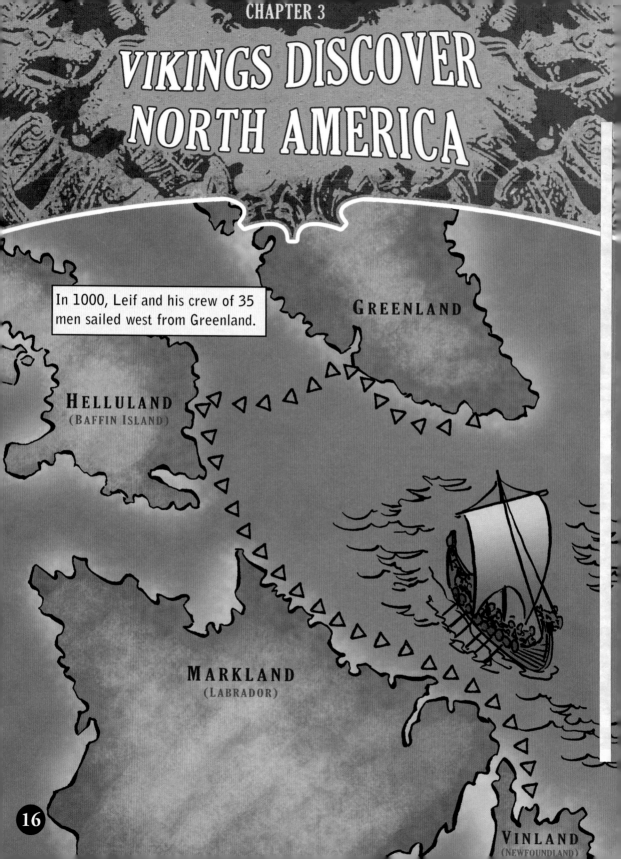

In 1000, Leif and his crew of 35 men sailed west from Greenland.

GREENLAND

HELLULAND
(BAFFIN ISLAND)

MARKLAND
(LABRADOR)

VINLAND
(NEWFOUNDLAND)

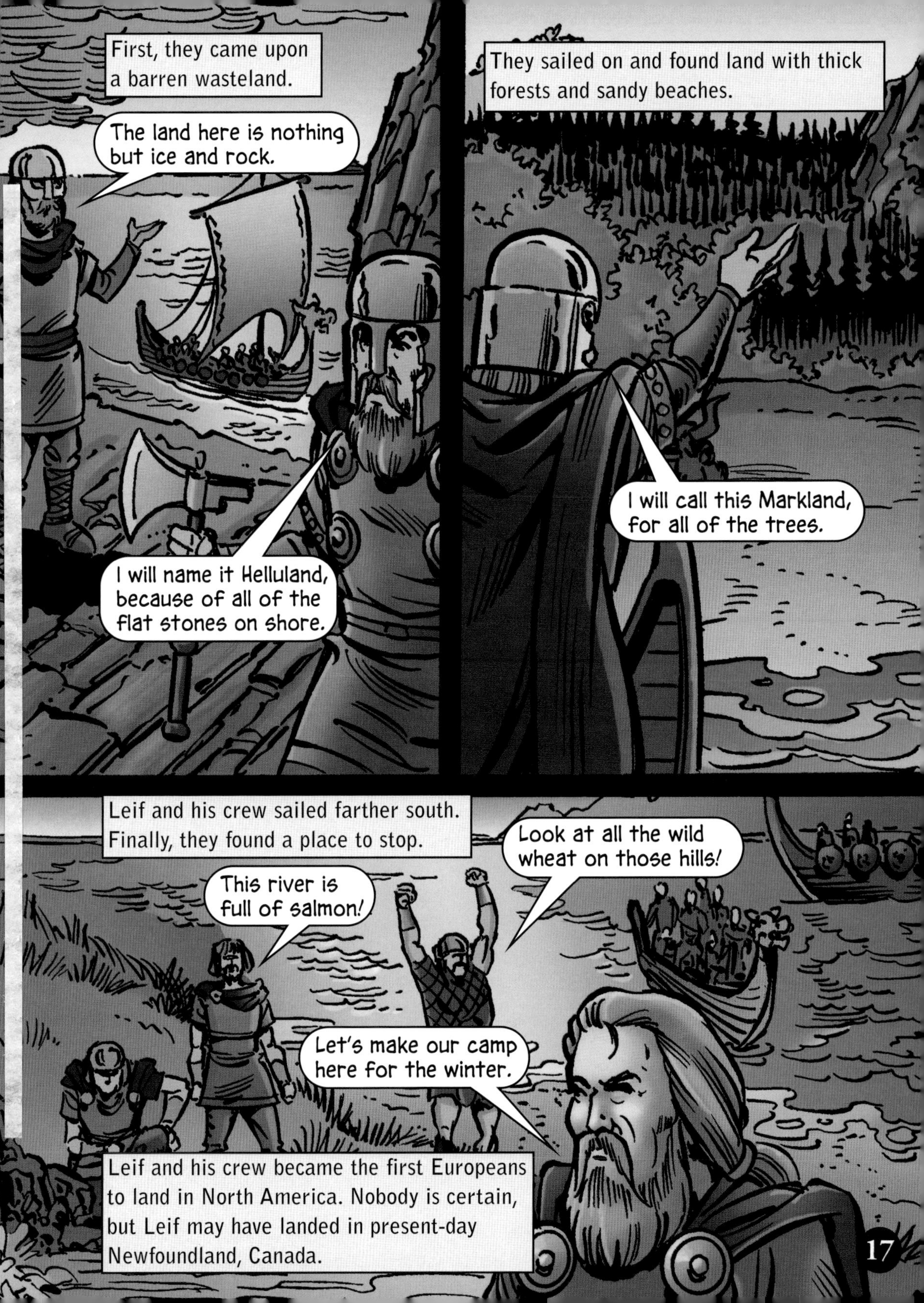
First, they came upon a barren wasteland.
The land here is nothing but ice and rock.
I will name it Helluland, because of all of the flat stones on shore.
They sailed on and found land with thick forests and sandy beaches.
I will call this Markland, for all of the trees.
Leif and his crew sailed farther south. Finally, they found a place to stop.
This river is full of salmon!
Look at all the wild wheat on those hills!
Let's make our camp here for the winter.
Leif and his crew became the first Europeans to land in North America. Nobody is certain, but Leif may have landed in present-day Newfoundland, Canada.

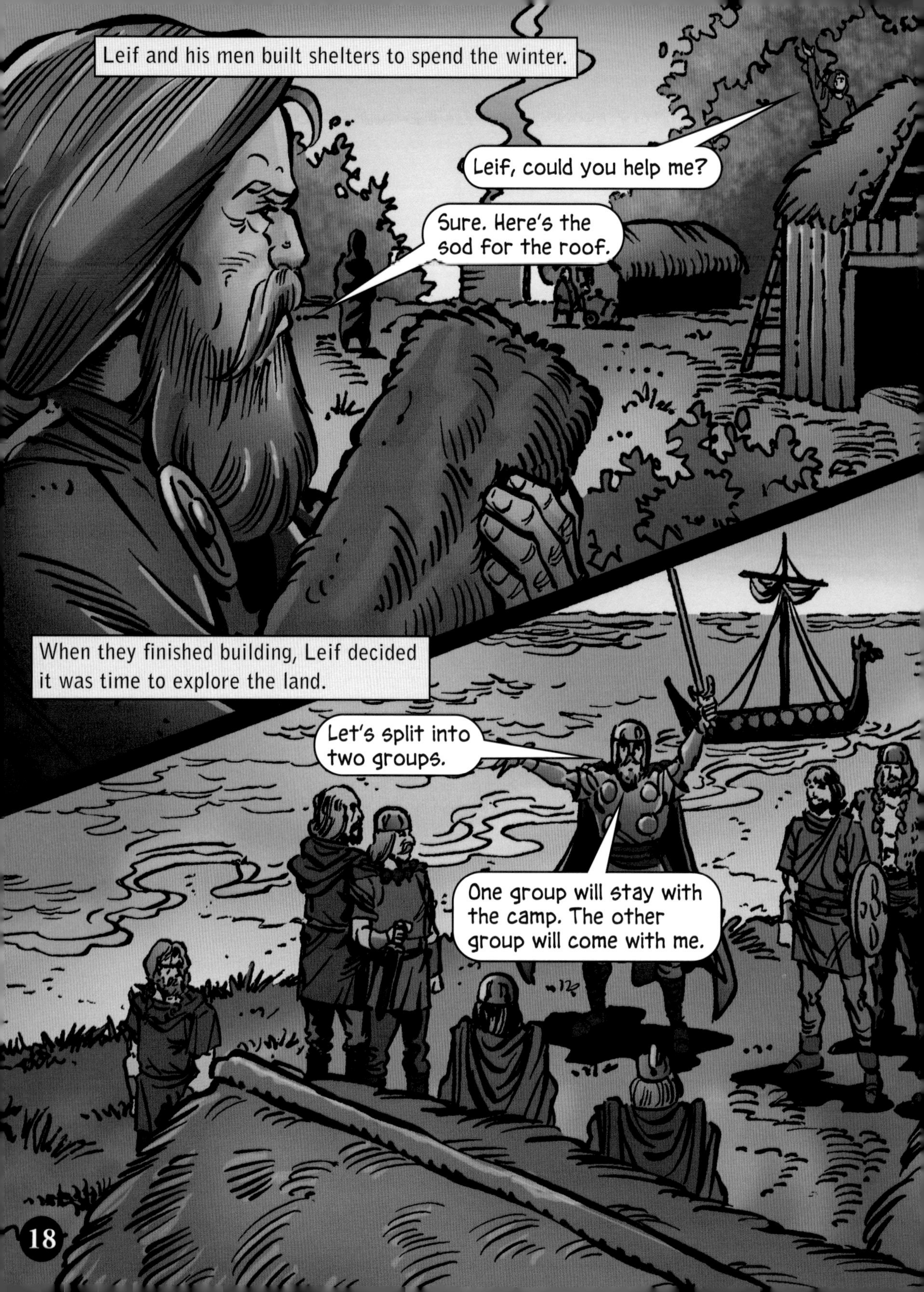

Leif and his men built shelters to spend the winter.
Leif, could you help me?
Sure. Here's the sod for the roof.
When they finished building, Leif decided it was time to explore the land.
Let's split into two groups.
One group will stay with the camp. The other group will come with me.

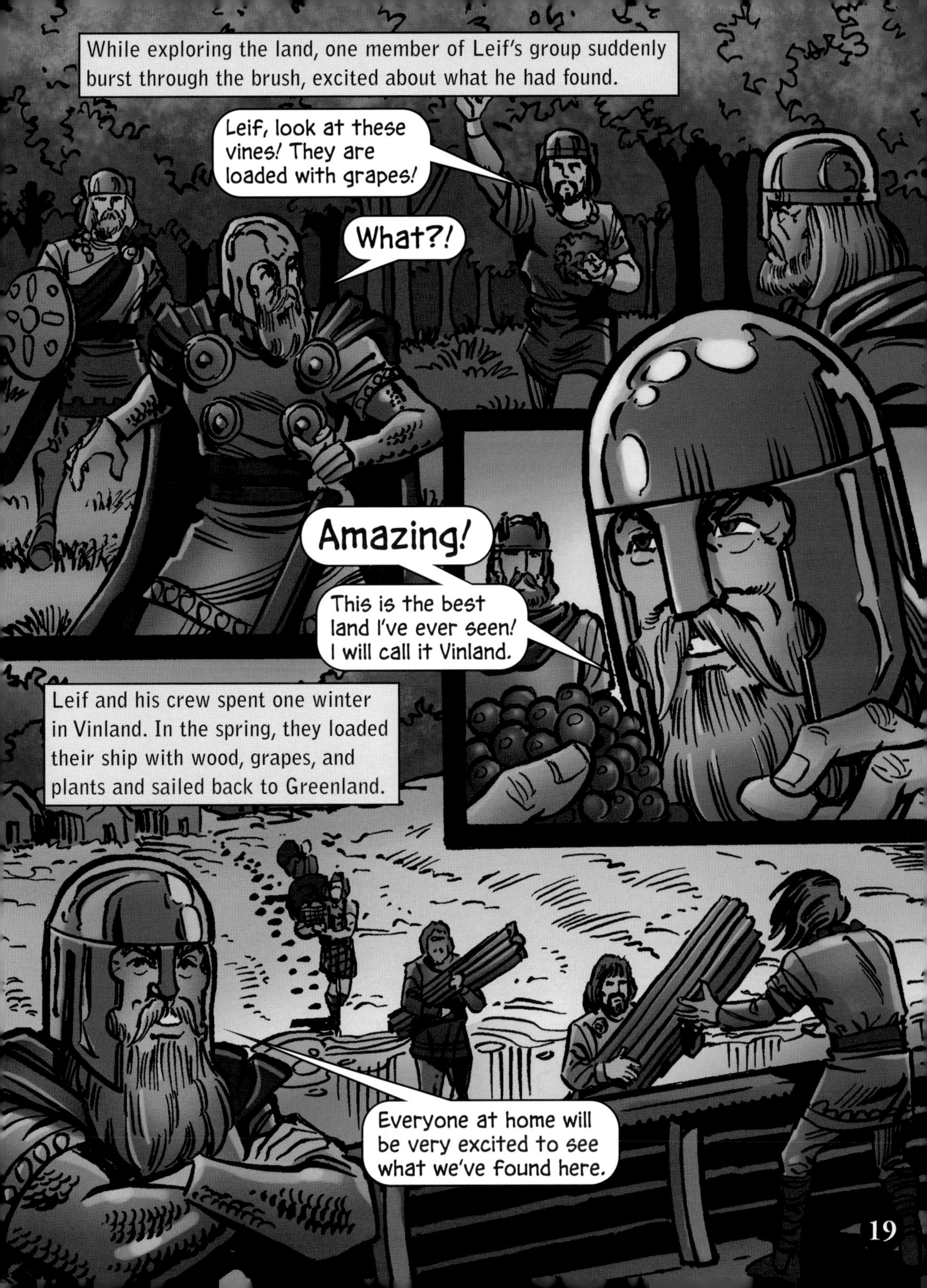
While exploring the land, one member of Leif's group suddenly burst through the brush, excited about what he had found.
Leif, look at these vines! They are loaded with grapes!
What?!
Amazing!
This is the best land I've ever seen! I will call it Vinland.
Leif and his crew spent one winter in Vinland. In the spring, they loaded their ship with wood, grapes, and plants and sailed back to Greenland.
Everyone at home will be very excited to see what we've found here.

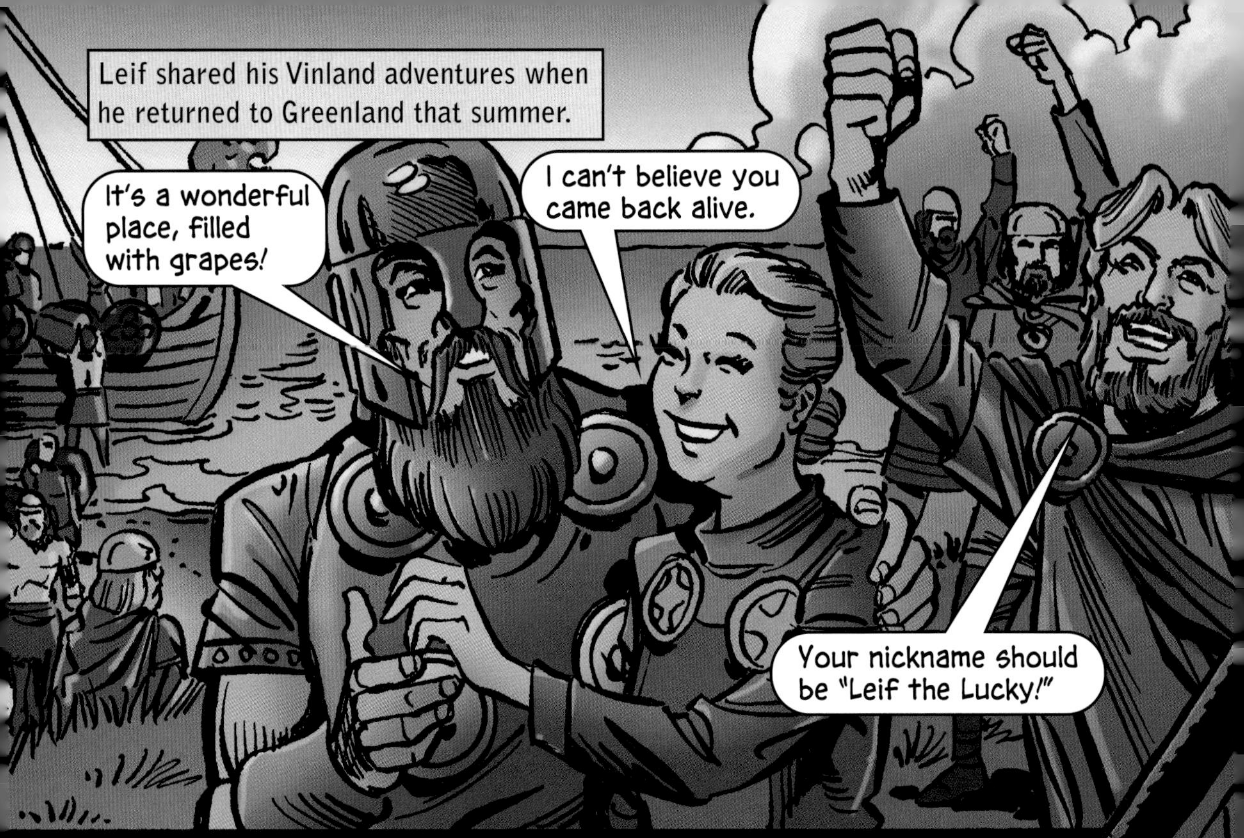
Leif shared his Vinland adventures when he returned to Greenland that summer.
It's a wonderful place, filled with grapes!
I can't believe you came back alive.
Your nickname should be "Leif the Lucky!"

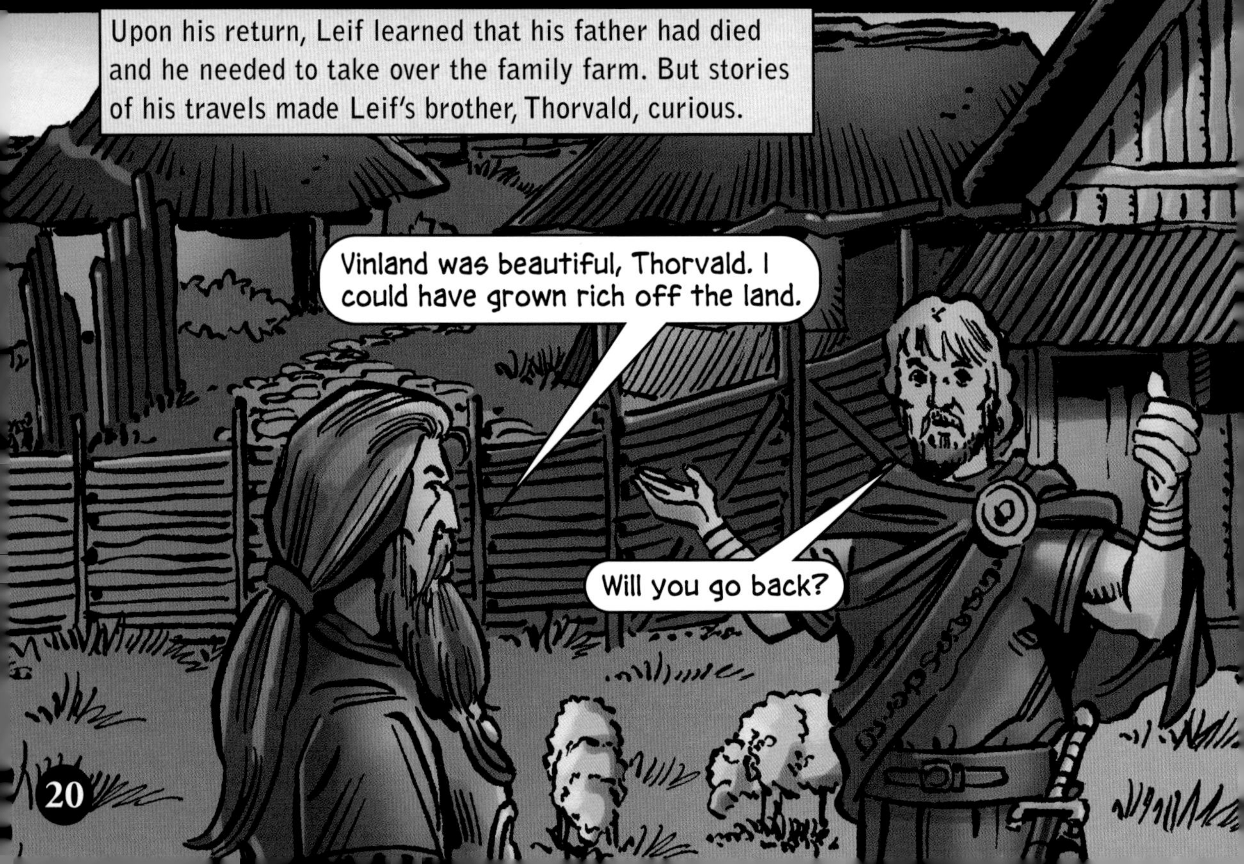
Upon his return, Leif learned that his father had died and he needed to take over the family farm. But stories of his travels made Leif's brother, Thorvald, curious.
Vinland was beautiful, Thorvald. I could have grown rich off the land.
Will you go back?

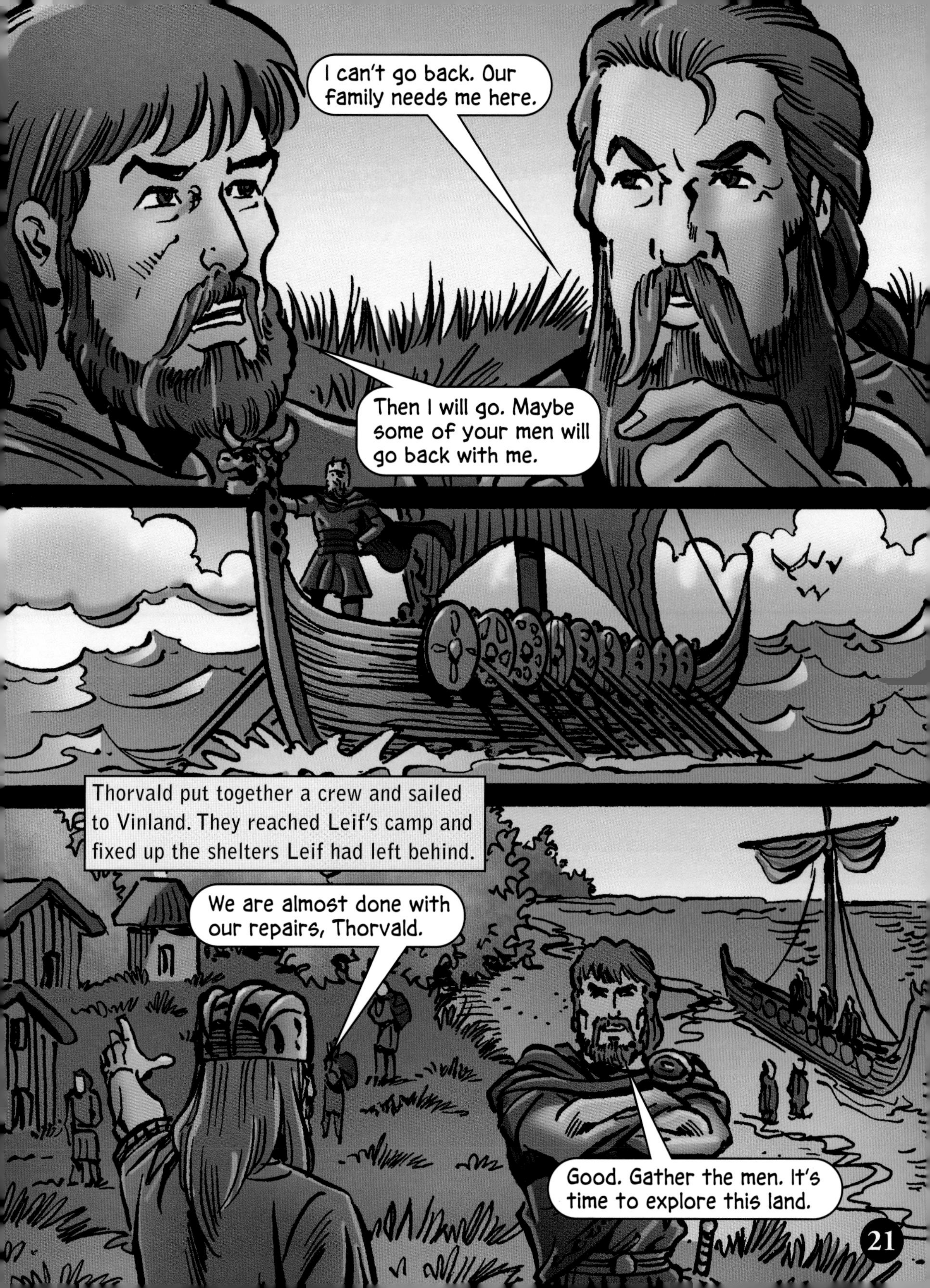
I can't go back. Our family needs me here.
Then I will go. Maybe some of your men will go back with me.
Thorvald put together a crew and sailed to Vinland. They reached Leif's camp and fixed up the shelters Leif had left behind.
We are almost done with our repairs, Thorvald.
Good. Gather the men. It's time to explore this land.

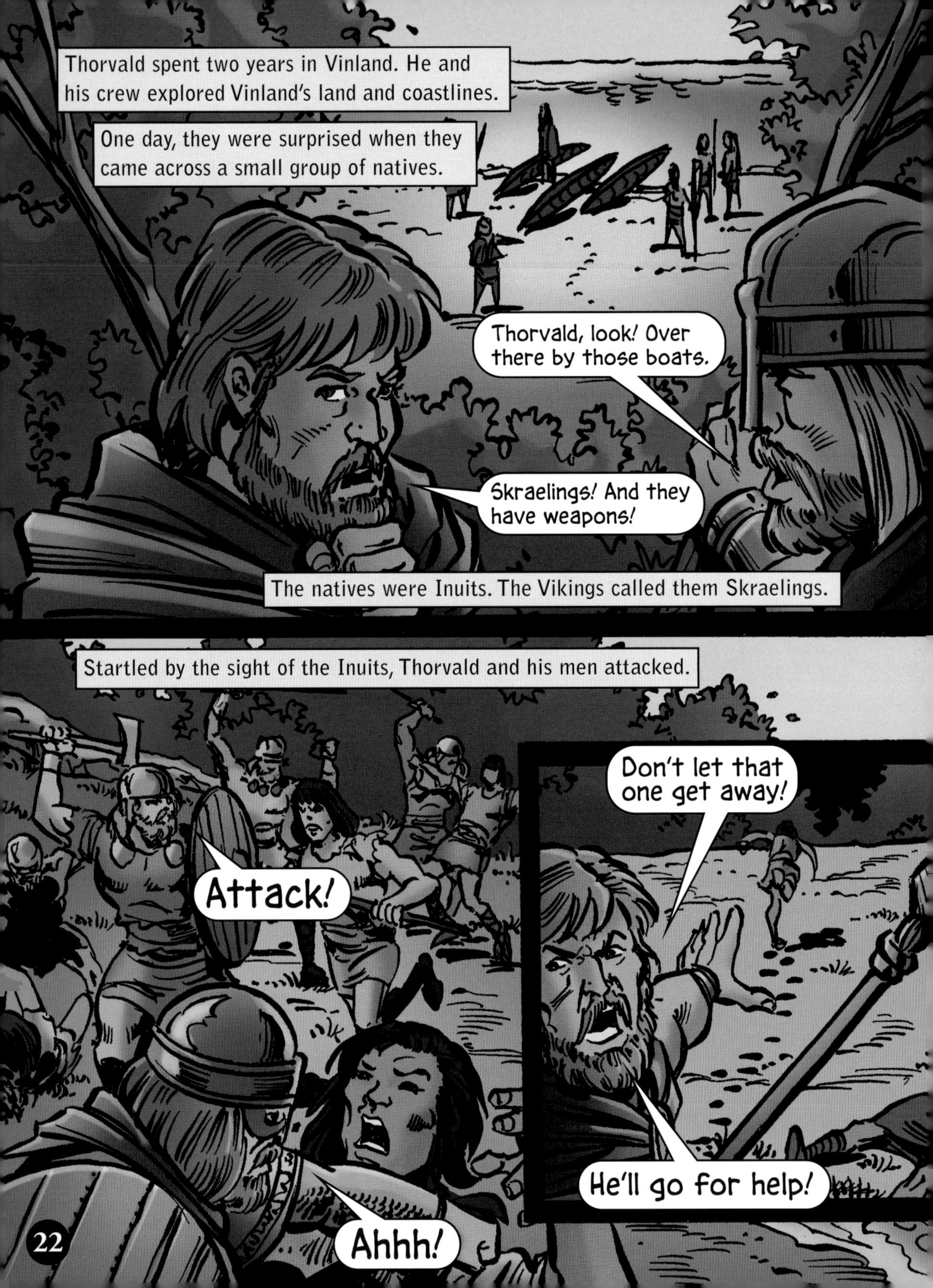

Thorvald spent two years in Vinland. He and his crew explored Vinland's land and coastlines.
One day, they were surprised when they came across a small group of natives.
Thorvald, look! Over there by those boats.
Skraelings! And they have weapons!
The natives were Inuits. The Vikings called them Skraelings.
Startled by the sight of the Inuits, Thorvald and his men attacked.
Attack!
Ahhh!
Don't let that one get away!
He'll go for help!

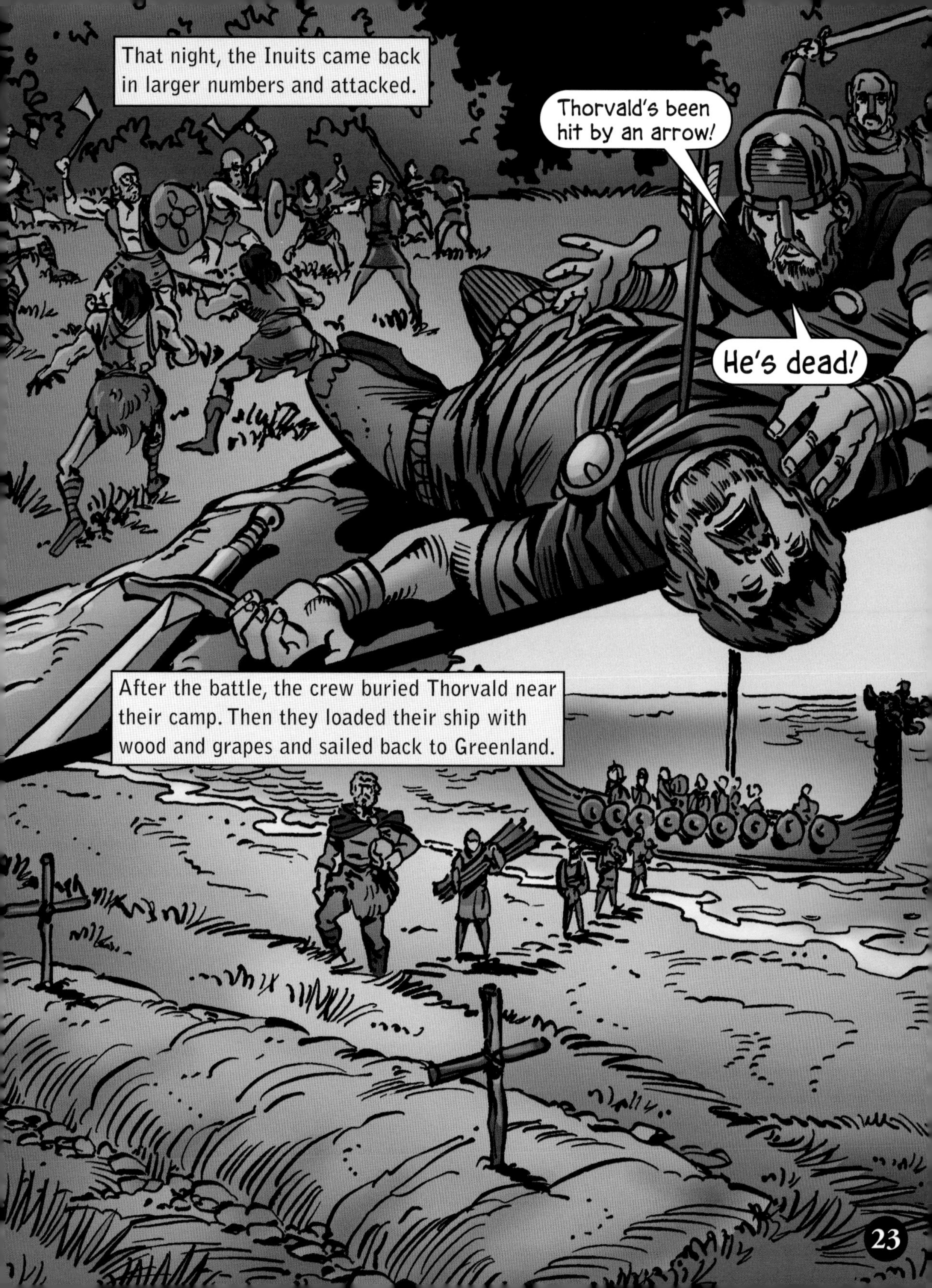
That night, the Inuits came back in larger numbers and attacked.
Thorvald's been hit by an arrow!
He's dead!
After the battle, the crew buried Thorvald near their camp. Then they loaded their ship with wood and grapes and sailed back to Greenland.

CHAPTER 4

THE LAST VIKINGS IN NORTH AMERICA

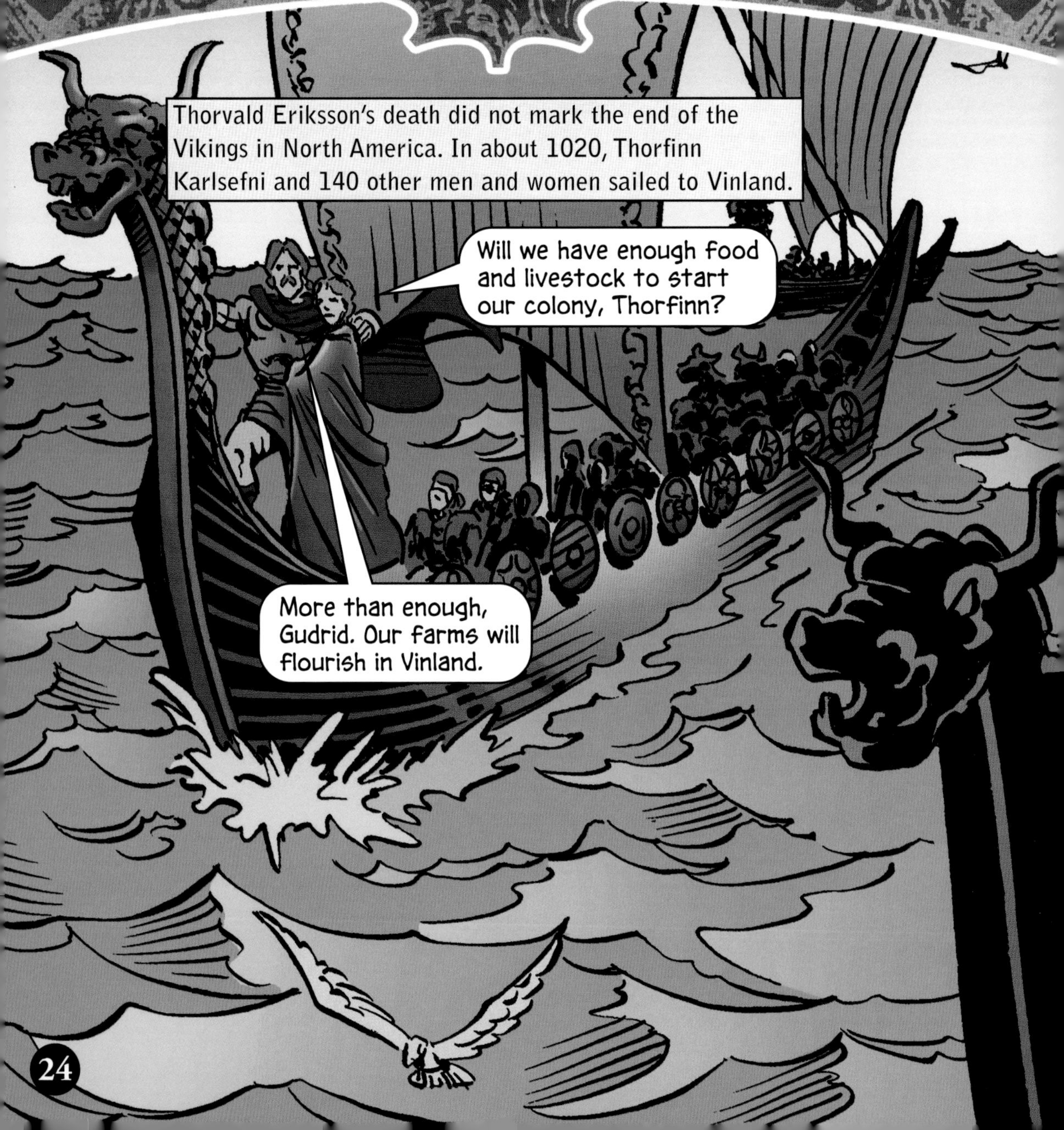
Thorvald Eriksson's death did not mark the end of the Vikings in North America. In about 1020, Thorfinn Karlsefni and 140 other men and women sailed to Vinland.
Will we have enough food and livestock to start our colony, Thorfinn?
More than enough, Gudrid. Our farms will flourish in Vinland.

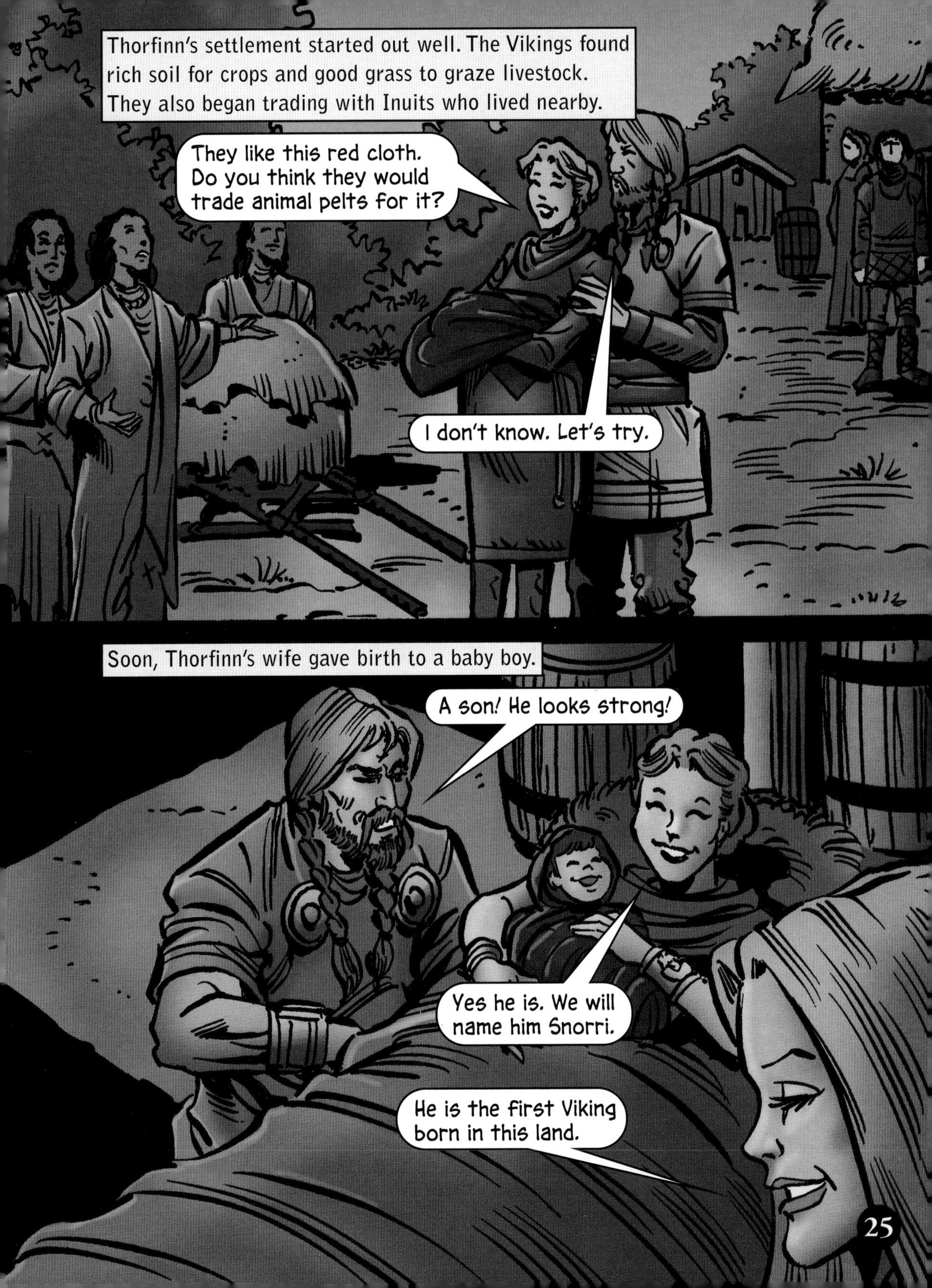
Thorfinn's settlement started out well. The Vikings found rich soil for crops and good grass to graze livestock. They also began trading with Inuits who lived nearby.
They like this red cloth. Do you think they would trade animal pelts for it?
I don't know. Let's try.
Soon, Thorfinn's wife gave birth to a baby boy.
A son! He looks strong!
Yes he is. We will name him Snorri.
He is the first Viking born in this land.

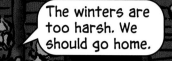

Unfortunately, Thorfinn's good fortune in Vinland didn't last. After three years, problems began to arise within the settlement.

The winters are too harsh. We should go home.

There are too many men here and not enough women.

The Skraelings are angry because we won't trade our weapons to them.

We can make this settlement work!

Finally, trade with the Inuits broke down. The natives became angry with the Vikings and attacked the settlement.

Our iron weapons are much better than bows and spears!

Yes, but they do us no good if we can't get close enough to use them.

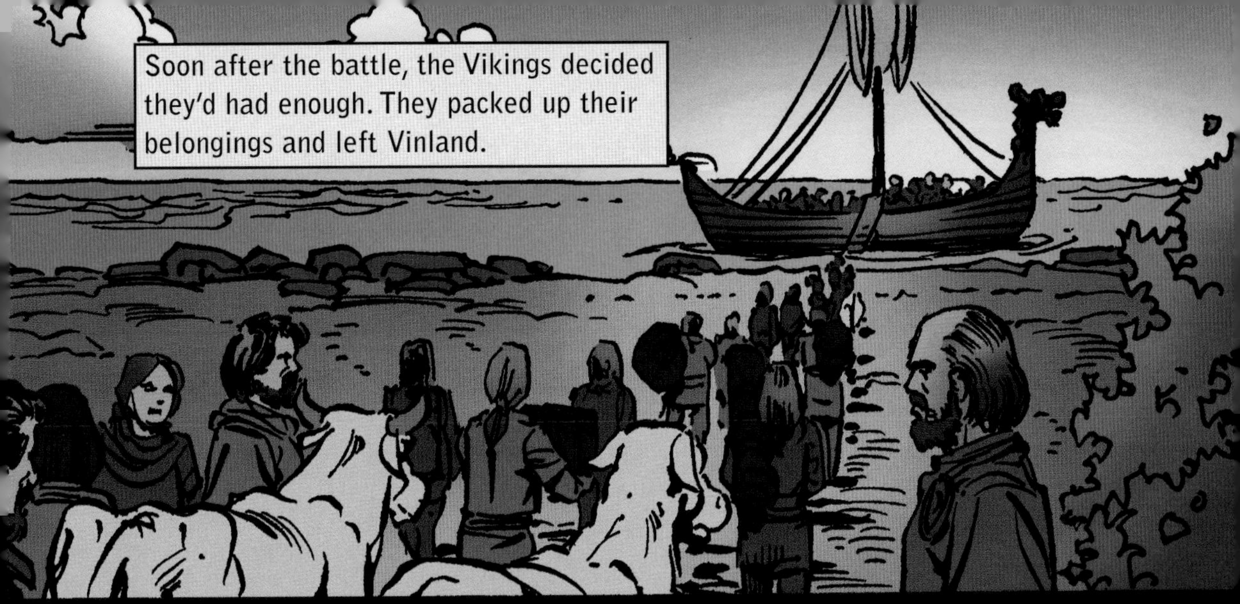
Soon after the battle, the Vikings decided they'd had enough. They packed up their belongings and left Vinland.

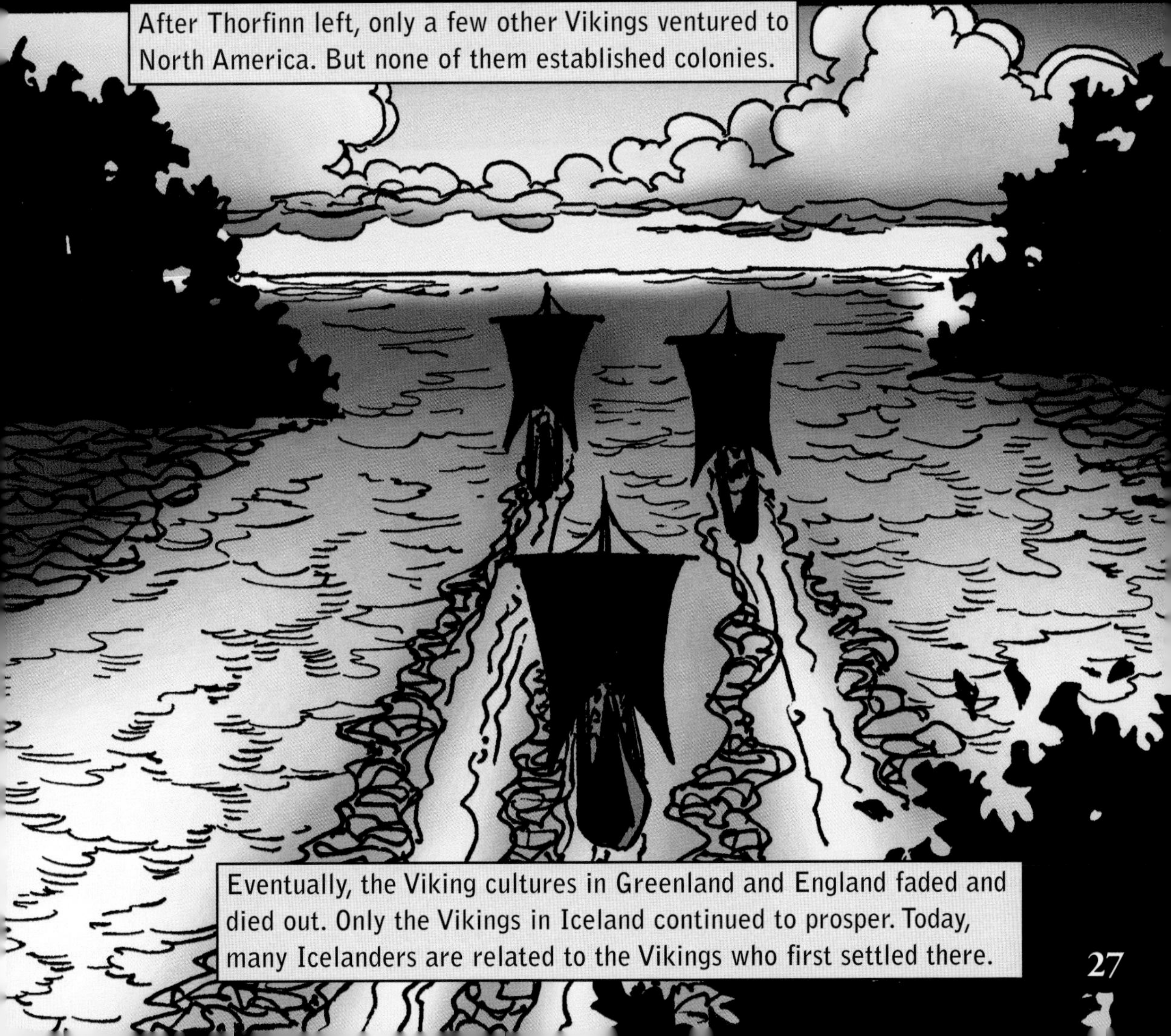
After Thorfinn left, only a few other Vikings ventured to North America. But none of them established colonies.
Eventually, the Viking cultures in Greenland and England faded and died out. Only the Vikings in Iceland continued to prosper. Today, many Icelanders are related to the Vikings who first settled there.

THE VIKINGS

 Vikings often are shown with horned helmets, but the helmets they wore didn't actually have horns.

 Many Vikings had descriptive names, such as Harald Fair-Hair, Svein Forkbeard, and Harald Bluetooth.

 Four days of the week are named for Germanic or Viking gods. Tuesday is named for Tyr. Wednesday is named after Odin. Thursday is named for the god Thor. Friday is named after Frey.

 Around 1500, the Viking settlements in Greenland died out. No one knows exactly why. The Vikings may have died of disease or used up all the natural resources.

 In the 1960s, archaeologists found the remains of a Viking settlement at L'Anse aux Meadows in Newfoundland, Canada. This site is the only known Viking settlement in North America.

The Vikings traveled not only west but also east to Russia and the Middle East. Along the way, they traded goods, weapons, and silver with the people they met. Much of the silver the Vikings had was made into jewelry. Both men and women wore silver rings, necklaces, and broaches.

 Vikings traveled on land using horses, wagons, skis, and sleds. They even made ice skates out of animal bones.

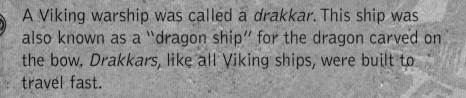 A Viking warship was called a *drakkar*. This ship was also known as a "dragon ship" for the dragon carved on the bow. *Drakkars*, like all Viking ships, were built to travel fast.

The Vikings created the earliest form of parliamentary government in Europe. Known as the Althing, this outdoor meeting allowed free farmers to voice problems and discuss laws.

GLOSSARY

banish (BAN-ish)—to send someone away from a place and order the person not to return

colony (KOL-uh-nee)—an area that has been settled by people from another country

fjord (fee-ORD)—a long, narrow inlet of ocean between high cliffs

flourish (FLUR-ish)—to grow and succeed

navigator (NAV-uh-gay-tuhr)—a person who uses maps, compasses, and the stars to guide a ship

plunder (PLUHN-dur)—to steal things by force

INTERNET SITES

FactHound offers a safe, fun way to find Internet sites related to this book. All of the sites on FactHound have been researched by our staff.

Here's how:

1. Visit *www.facthound.com*
2. Type in this special code **0736849742** for age-appropriate sites. Or enter a search word related to this book for a more general search.
3. Click on the **Fetch It** button.

FactHound will fetch the best sites for you!

READ MORE

Chrisp, Peter. *The Vikings.* Strange Histories. Chicago: Raintree, 2003.

Gallagher, Jim. *Viking Explorers.* Explorers of New Worlds. Philadelphia: Chelsea House, 2001.

Glaser, Jason. *Leif Eriksson.* Fact Finders: Biographies. Mankato, Minn.: Capstone Press, 2005.

Hatt, Christine. *The Viking World.* Excavating the Past. Chicago: Heinemann, 2005.

Hopkins, Andrea. *Viking Longships.* The Viking Library. New York: PowerKids Press, 2002.

BIBLIOGRAPHY

Brent, Peter Ludwig. *The Viking Saga.* London: Weidenfeld and Nicolson, 1975.

Jones, Gwyn. *A History of the Vikings.* London: Oxford University Press, 2001.

Roesdahl, Else. *The Vikings.* Translated by Susan M. Margeson and Kirsten Williams. London: Penguin Books, 1998.

Sawyer, P. H. *The Oxford Illustrated History of the Vikings.* New York: Oxford University Press, 1997.

INDEX